Daniel —

Merci pour ton
support et ta belle
énergie !

Connie Robichaud.
le 18 octobre 2014.

KEEP IT SIMPLE, SPIRIT

Simple Practices for Peace of Mind,
Loving Yourself, and a Joyful Life!

CONNIE ROBICHAUD

BALBOA.
PRESS

A DIVISION OF HAY HOUSE

Balboa Press books may be ordered through booksellers or by contacting:

Balboa Press
A Division of Hay House
1663 Liberty Drive
Bloomington, IN 47403
www.balboapress.com
1 (877) 407-4847

Because of the dynamic nature of the Internet, any web addresses or
links contained in this book may have changed since publication and may
no longer be valid. The views expressed in this work are solely those
of the author and do not necessarily reflect the views of the publisher,
and the publisher hereby disclaims any responsibility for them.

The author of this book does not dispense medical advice or prescribe the
use of any technique as a form of treatment for physical, emotional, or medical
problems without the advice of a physician, either directly or indirectly. The
intent of the author is only to offer information of a general nature to help you
in your quest for emotional and spiritual well-being. In the event you use any
of the information in this book for yourself, which is your constitutional right,
the author and the publisher assume no responsibility for your actions.

Any people depicted in stock imagery provided by Thinkstock are models,
and such images are being used for illustrative purposes only.
Certain stock imagery © Thinkstock.

Printed in the United States of America.

ISBN: 978-1-4525-9458-3 (sc)
ISBN: 978-1-4525-9459-0 (e)

Library of Congress Control Number: 2014905112

Balboa Press rev. date: 04/10/2014

DEDICATIONS & ACKNOWLEDGMENTS

God…
For Divine Planning and leading me on the right path,

Ron Robichaud…
My husband, for keeping me on the path (when I de-railed),

Chérisse Robichaud…
Our youngest daughter, thanks for your creative art on this cover,

Lisanne Robichaud…
Our eldest daughter and loving, special teacher in so many ways,

Family and Friends…

*My Acadian hometown Municipality of
Clare and Annapolis Valley, NS*
Thank you all for your support!

Teachers, Therapists, and Friends in Toronto…
Thank you for reaching out and being authentic.
You have touched my life deeply…more than you realize!

Special Dedications to Kindred Spirits:
Chris Johnson, I know you are still supervising me.

Maria Jankovic, for your presence in my life…Namaste!

Special Thanks…
Dorothy & Basile for being the best parents!
Randy for allowing me to feel and see life through your eyes!

CONTENTS

PREFACE

Simple Practices to Peace of Mind, Loving Yourself, and a Joyful Life!

Life used to be simple and uncomplicated. Life now is chaotic and stressful for most people. You can make your life much simpler by dealing with issues of the heart and spirit.

I believe that if you are currently dealing with emotional pain such as grief, anger, shame and fear (to name but a few), then more than likely you are exhausting yourself trying to repress these emotions with eating disorders, substance or alcohol abuse, overworking, numbing out with television or web surfing. All these patterns can be healed when we tend to heal our Inner Child, or inner Spirit. We can find our way back to wholeness and wellness by healing from the inside-out.

I also believe that if this pain is not released through therapy, it may manifest in chronic physical pain or diseases. Tap into your Inner Child energy, to avoid a tantrum!

Obesity is a major health issue in society today. Let me ask you one question: *How do you feed yourself*:

- ♥ Physically – eating real, wholesome food
- ♥ Mentally – applying coping skills to relieve stress and anxiety
- ♥ Emotionally – releasing old beliefs and patterns, or *baggage*

♥ Spiritually – addressing internal messages of your Inner Child

This book is for you, if:

♥ You are *ready* to take responsibility for your life.
♥ You want simple, effective techniques to heal your mental, emotional, physical and spiritual health.
♥ You allow the release of emotional baggage and old beliefs.

INTRODUCTION

Keep It Simple...Spirit is meant to enlighten and awaken you into awareness. At the very least, it is meant to entertain you, and perhaps you will gain a few insights in becoming a more empowered individual.

Like you, I've had my share of ups and downs. I've lived with 3 generations of mental illness with immediate family members. I've dealt with the drama of this illness as I watched from my ringside seat of life. I tried methods to block, resist, repress or deny the emotions that would rise up – all to no avail!

Then in 2010, a series of events led me to transform my life. I wanted to assist people in a different way. I wanted to teach people how to cope better with stress, and how to become excited about their lives. My passion soon revealed itself, by assisting others in finding their own inner peace. *Keep It Simple, Spirit* is a result of that inner passion.

This book is simple, and to the point.

This book contains simple coping methods, tips and techniques that can relieve stress and alleviate anxiety, understand your Spirit better, and assist you in creating a more joyful life. It is a lighthearted view of how simple life can be, if you just let yourself *be* more...with yourself, your partner, your children, your extended family, and friends, even your pets!

All too often we are not present to life. We are human *beings*, but we have become human *doings*, trying to squeeze more time out of each day. We are constantly distracted; we think that by multitasking we will achieve more, when in fact we need to spend more time just *being*.

I designed this book so that each chapter was short and simple. I wanted it to be practical, so that you could read a few chapters while sitting on the plane, or just before bedtime, and carry it in your pocketbook or backpack as a reference guide.

This book is a tool that is intended to guide you with humor and compassion, so you don't take yourself too seriously. With the variety of exercises I have inserted in this book, you will get to know yourself better as a whole person: physically, mentally, emotionally and spiritually. The only thing I ask is that you be *present* to the process and allow the release of whatever needs to be released. Life is about the journey, not a race to the destination. Be patient and loving to yourself.

This book is not a substitute for treatment from a professional. It can be complimentary to other treatments, either clinical or holistic, which you may be receiving now. If at any point you feel emotionally or mentally overwhelmed or unstable, please seek professional help. I am available for private sessions in person, by telephone, or by Skype, if you choose me as your therapist. Asking for help is an act of courage. Therapy is a gift to your spirit.

I also have a CD of meditations and reflections with personal messages from me to you, to wrap up the whole energy and essence of this book. There are other available CDs as well, including this book in audio format. All versions are available on my web page: www.therapy3.org Thank you.

Let's put the *fun* back in dys*fun*ction. Are you ready? Then buckle up for the journey!

THE STORY OF LITTLE SPIRIT

Once upon a time, there was a Little Spirit who was afraid of going into the deep, dark forest. She looked up at the dark sky, and called upon the Great Spirit, and shared her fears. "I'm so afraid of going into that dark forest all by myself", Little Spirit said, her lip quivering. "But if I don't go, I will not be able to gather food, and I am very hungry."

The Great Spirit gently spoke to Little Spirit in the warm, gentle breeze. "Little Spirit, you are never alone, I am always with you. I will place courage in your heart and purpose in your mind. I will lovingly guide you along the way. Just do your very best, Little Spirit, and I will take care of the rest." And when Great Spirit spoke that last word, the dark clouds parted, and the sun's bright rays illuminated a path in the dark forest for Little Spirit to follow safely. - Connie Robichaud

Reflection:

Can you relate to the fears that Little Spirit has in this story? The Little Spirit in this story is similar to our Inner Child that resides in our own hearts. Our internal Inner Child is the emotional part of ourselves that has been wounded and needs to be loved and nurtured by our Inner Adult, similar to the Great Spirit.

This story can also have a spiritual connection, if you wish to see it that way. Either way, you are on the right path.

1

Often it is fear that keeps us stuck and unable to face our own darkness. Fear can also be a strong force for positive change in our lives as well. This is similar to the sun's rays shining through that dark forest.

By embracing your darkness as well as your light, you become whole again. It is not possible to destroy fear, but to move though it with courage in our hearts and purpose in our minds, like Little Spirit.

So summon up that courage and move through the fear, one thing at a time. Start with small changes, and celebrate the successes along the way. Each success will build your self-esteem and confidence, and allow you to face the bigger changes you need to make in your life. Good luck, may the Great Spirit guide your way to the light!

My Notes...

3

MY POWERFUL A-TEAM...
AND YOURS TOO!

Like Little Spirit, I know I have a powerful A-Team that support and guide me in every moment of my life, consisting of angels, spirits and guides. And so do you! We are all born with at least one guardian angel by our side.

I wasn't always aware of their presence. I have a spirit guide that has been with me since I was 3 years of age. I feel he came in at a time in my life when my home life was getting really chaotic and he felt I needed support. As my purpose became clearer these past few years, it became apparent that my team needed growing. When I was doing my studies in Toronto, I sometimes felt lonely, but I never felt alone. I knew that by connecting to my spiritual guides, I would feel safe and supported. Carl G. Jung, Swiss psychotherapist and psychiatrist and Robert Assagioli, Italian psychiatrist, also worked with spirit guides, so I am in good company.

For those of you who prefer not to connect to your spirits, please do not judge yourselves. You may not be ready to do so just yet. That is perfectly fine. My God-given gifts are clairvoyance, clairsentience and intuitive empathy. *Clairvoyance* is the ability to *see* things that are not visible with our physical eyes. I observe with my third eye, which is located on the forehead (we all have one), just above the eyebrows. At times I see spirits, dead people, walking about at funerals. At times it is like a movie playing right in front of me, and if I turn away and look back, the images are still there. I envision some relatives and guests at the funeral parlour or during the church services. It is such a beautiful sight to behold that I am often brought to tears by the angelic sights. I feel this must be as close to heaven as I can possibly be in my human experience. I've often wished they would invent a telepathic projector so everyone could see what I see.

Clairsentience is the ability to *feel* energy from people, places and objects. I regarded this ability as a curse or a burden most of my life, because I did not know how to cope with it, and it affected me adversely. I always felt emotionally and physically drained, and was not equipped to deal with life in a healthy way. Now with coping skills and techniques, I feel life in a different way. I ensure I am well grounded if I attend large groups that may draw on my energy. It is a continuous process.

If I am adversely affected by a person or event, I know intuitively that something is not right, because of the feelings or thoughts that are popping into my mind or my body. I take time to clear my energy field, and then I connect with my spiritual power, bring it down through my spine (chakras or energy centres) and ground it very firmly into the earth. It takes less than 5 minutes of my time and my energy flows naturally once more. This exercise is very empowering, because you become accountable to how you deal with your own emotional and mental health. If at any point you feel *overwhelmed* with life events, please consider receiving counselling from a professional therapist.

My definition of *intuitive empathy* is a sense of putting myself in the other person's shoes, but being objective in the process. In other words, I briefly go into a person's energy field but I don't stay there. I want to empathize with the other person, but I cannot assist them if I get stuck in that energy too. I cannot help others if I get stuck in their pain, and this is why I need to remain objective to their issues.

I also want to make a point here by saying that I cannot *force* any spirit to come forward. Spirits will come forward when they feel their loved ones need comforting and to let them know they are doing well. Some people know me as a *medium*, although I am more comfortable being called an *intuitive*. Everyone has the ability to sense other people's energies, but have forgotten how to do so.

When a client sits with me, I ensure they are honored in the most sacred ways. I clear the energy of the space prior to our session, using a combination of these methods: smudging, chanting, sound (tuning forks or bells), prayer, drumming, dancing, to name a few. I always summon all my guides and my Higher Power and flood the room with the pure white light of love. I also light a candle in my client's honour. I pray for guidance and support in speaking my truth for this client so they may do their healing in their own way. I don't heal people; they heal themselves when the time is right for them. I support them with tools, techniques and the guidance they need, but they need to be ready for the healing. Everything happens in Divine Timing.

I use my gifts of clairvoyance, clairsentience, intuitive empathy as well as active listening and observing your body language. I also listen to the silence between the words, because often times the truth of your pain is in the silence.

Prior to becoming a psychotherapist, I was too sensitive to the energy of others in general. I felt I had no control (much like in my childhood), so I created an unconscious barrier or armour to shield myself against bad emotions, when in fact there are no bad emotions; they are just *energy in motion*. Going through life with a shield is exhausting work; once I could drop that shield, admit my truth, and deal with my emotions in a healthy way, I felt a freedom and peace I never knew existed. I continue to process my emotions in various ways so that I can be the clearest channel for guidance and healing, not only for my clients, but in my personal relationships as well.

It takes courage to admit that you feel different from other individuals. It has been challenging for me to admit in having these God-given gifts! My passion to assist others overpowers any fear I need to overcome. All I ask is that you become present to your own life. You have been granted the gift of life – how will you use the remainder of it? Hiding behind a shield is exhausting, and shedding all those layers of emotional baggage is exhilarating! Choose to become an active player in your own healing journey.

I have tried various methods, and the one I found that works best for clearing my energy and grounding me is on my compact disc under the title, "I AM". For the sensitive souls out there who have energetic challenges on a daily basis, I sincerely hope that this method works for you as well. I know it has worked amazingly well for me.

As for your own powerful A-team, call on them. You don't need to believe they exist just because I've told you they do. I do know they are very under-employed beings! They will come for assistance at any time of the day or night, because they don't need sleep and they don't have time schedules like we do on earth. Sit in silence and ask to feel their presence with a sound, a scent, or a feeling. Don't despair if you don't receive guidance right away, you are probably trying too hard. Just like the other exercises in this book, they work best when you let yourself release your expectations to the outcome, and open your heart and spirit to whatever needs to happen.

Just acknowledge them in your life, and thank them when they grant you assistance. You will be glad you did.

Reflection:

What are your opinions based on your life experiences? Do you believe in angels, guides, and spirits? Does this serve as a basis for your spirituality practices?

I encourage you to take a different perspective at your spiritual beliefs. Write down any thoughts you have regarding this subject, if you wish. Live with an open heart and spirit, and experience life to its fullest manifestation of richness and beauty. It truly is a sight to behold.

My Notes...

LET'S GET THIS PARTY STARTED!

This book is about a lot of things. It is based in spirituality, compassion, forgiveness and love on every level of your body, mind, spirit and emotional being.

I have added a little touch of humor inside these pages, in case you begin to take yourself too seriously. In fact, I would love to prepare you for the party of your life. Just think of all the people you would invite to your grand banquet of life! Reflect on all your loved ones, and how you have influenced them in their lives. Think of your extended family and friends who live far away, but with whom you still have contact occasionally. These people are all part of the circle of your life, and you have influenced everyone you have ever met in your life, in a small or big way.

Also think of the people you do not like, and reflect on how your life would be if you were able to forgive them for the wrongs you feel they have inflicted upon you. If you could forgive those people, think of how much positive energy you would gain by releasing that emotional baggage. No one can heal in negativity and stress. That is the reason the exercises in this book are heart-based and tend to your spirit; by relaxing your physical body you gradually open up the channels to receiving more healing for your spirit. That armour of protection becomes chipped away as the healing progresses over time.

Reflection:

With all these thoughts in mind, focus on a life that is less stressful, and more peaceful and joyful than it is now. What would that feel like? Do you think it would show on both the inside and the outside of your body? What does a peaceful person look and act like?

Take a few moments to sit back and reflect on how you would write an invitation to all those people you have loved, befriended, and influenced. What would the invitation say? I would suggest you invite everyone and their Little Spirits to the party, to make sure everyone has fun and do not get too serious. After all, this is your party!

My Notes...

THE BLAME GAME!

Do you enjoy playing games? Just invite that little Inner Child to come out to play with your Adult today. She or he has so much wisdom when you try to deal with affairs of the heart.

Do you currently feel or have you ever felt as if others are dealt all the good cards in the deck, and you are left with the jokers? Has this happened to the point that you didn't want to play cards anymore? Maybe you decided to have a little pity party of your own. Or perhaps you decided to play the Blame Game! Come on down!

If you have *never* felt this way, you are probably not human, and I would certainly love to meet you! You may tend to blame others when you don't get that promotion, when life doesn't feel fair, and when others seem to get all the lucky breaks. It is perfectly normal to feel this way occasionally, but it becomes an issue when it is a repeated pattern of behavior.

It is so much easier to blame others when things don't go quite the way you want. This behavior is really coming from your scared Inner Child. It is a pattern that your Inner Child adapted to protect him/herself. It is a defense mechanism. By placing high expectations on other people, not on yourself, you absolve any responsibility of being accountable for your own actions. Ouch! As an Adult, you need to be responsible for your own actions; there are ways of overcoming this behavior.

Whenever it began, and however it manifested in your life, you have the power to change it, now you are aware of it. You are giving away your power, and you need to reclaim it back!

You have the power to change your life for the better, no one else does. Like other support people in your life, I can guide you to the watering hole, but you must drink from the pool of water. It is a simple process, but it may not be easy, especially at first.

This process requires time and dedication on your part. Blame becomes a pattern in your life, and you become comfortable with that energy, just like any other pattern of behavior, such as denial, guilt, or anger, for example. It is a learned behavior which can be replaced with positive, healthy behavior. Allow yourself about 30 days to master one positive change. When you regress back to this old pattern, stop! Simply stated, you are acting out from your *wounded* Inner Child behavior; bring your Adult into the picture to ensure mature and responsible choices.

This new behavior program will take time to replace the old patterns. Forgive yourself when you regress; you are only human! With time, these positive changes will boost your self-esteem, and make your Adult more confident in making informed, responsible decisions.

Reflection:

Let's take your physical health, for example. Would you like to improve the way you physically look or feel? How will you achieve this? Can you begin an exercise program? If you can't afford a gym or exercise classes, there are plenty of free exercise routines on the internet, and various books and compact discs on lifestyle changes. Are you willing to start a walking program? When my children were small, I would exercise in my kitchen, while keeping a watchful eye on them as they played in the next room. I did not blame anyone else for having to exercise at home. It was an adult choice I made, in view of my life events at that time.

This brings me to the next point of making *adult* choices. When you place blame, you are acting from the perspective of your *wounded* Inner Child, not your Adult. Once you heal and release the emotions around the blame, you are healing your Inner Child, or the emotional part of your heart. They both need to be present, because your *healed* Inner Child will ensure your Adult has fun!

Keep track of when your energy levels are the highest. If you are not a morning person, then don't set yourself up for failure and set the clock for 6am! Make *realistic goals* to ensure your success. Perhaps you can walk 20 minutes at noon if you have a day job, and this will lower stress as well. Let your body's wisdom inform you what you need to do. Reflect on ways to improve your health both now and in the coming months.

In the notes section that follows, jot down what you want to achieve in 12 months. Then back track month by month to visualize your progress, until you reach your current month. Small changes over the course of 12 months can add up to big changes! What can you do differently? Think of one small change that would begin to shift your health in a better way. There is always room for improvement. And remember, only do one change at a time. Keeping track with a journal or marking your progress on a calendar provides a visual aspect for you.

Enlist the assistance of someone who can coach you in your journey if you can't do it alone. Asking for support is a sign of strength, not weakness! Whenever you reach a goal, really *ground* it by acknowledging that success, because it is *significant*. Treat yourself with a nature walk, a pedicure, a message, crank up the music and dance or sing, or invite a friend for tea or coffee. At the very least, give yourself a hug as a reward; your Inner Child will love you for it!

My point is there are always small changes you can do, when you are truthful with yourself. The transition to a new way of doing things is often challenging, but the rewards are many. You need to take back your power in making positive life choices; no one else can do that for you. You are the catalyst for change.

For the moment, begin and end every day with an *attitude of gratitude*. You cannot be miserable and grateful in the same moment. And being grateful for what you have *now* puts you in a positive state of mind. The following chapter is dedicated to this very subject, because it is so important in your life. Remember to celebrate the small changes or successes along the way. Keep trying. Your beautiful Inner Child is definitely worth the time and effort.

My Notes...

ATTITUDE OF GRATITUDE

What are you grateful for in your life? We can all be grateful for something big or small. No matter what our current situation, we can always find something that is a blessing. Something that may seem insignificant can be a hidden blessing in your life. Because it is worth repeating, *it is not possible to be miserable and grateful at the same time*. They are at opposite ends of the feeling spectrum and cannot be felt simultaneously. For example, if you are *truly* grateful for food in your fridge, you cannot be miserable because you don't have lettuce. And this scenario unfolds for every area of your life. If you allow yourself to be truly grateful for the small and big things in your life, you will begin to attract more positive energy into your life. People don't like to hang around with negative, ungrateful people, but are attracted to positive and grateful ones.

I've seen seemingly poor people who were very happy, because they were grateful for the things they had, even if it seemed like very little to someone else's eyes. They focused on their blessings instead of the lack in their lives. They did not measure themselves against someone else's expectations of being grateful and happy, because this comes from ego, not from loving gratitude.

Reflection:

Take a moment to close your eyes, and bring your attention to your heart. You can be grateful that your precious heart is beating without being told, every day, month after month. You can be grateful for the gift of breath, which is indeed the gift of life. When we were born, we took our first breaths and will continue to do so until our last day on earth. Have a pen ready to jot down things you are grateful for at the end of this breathing exercise. Just writing a few things in this book will serve to remind you of the blessings you have in your life.

Use a 4-second count for each intake and each release of breath and hold 4 seconds between each breath. Inhale through your nose and exhale through your mouth.

1. To a count of 4 seconds: Begin by taking 1 deep breath through your nose, into your belly (see your belly rise up), slowly up, until you completely fill up your lungs.
2. Hold the breath for 4 seconds.
3. To a count of 4 seconds, release your breath through your mouth, from the top of your lungs, and lastly from your belly, expelling all the air.
4. Hold for 4 seconds.
5. Repeat 3 times, from step #1.

An attitude of gratitude keeps us in the present moment. When you awaken in the morning and before you sleep at night, think of at least one thing for which you are grateful. By focusing on your blessings, you will attract more blessings into your life. Tomorrow's destiny is shaped by what you do today.

My Notes...

THE QUEEN – OR KING - OF DENIAL (NOT THE NILE)

I often mention that it's healthy to laugh *with* ourselves, not *at* ourselves. And I sincerely believe this to be true. Our bodies are *listening* to what we are telling them. Scientific research has proven this to be true. The messages that we repeatedly tell ourselves are absorbed by our body's energy and recorded in our DNA codes. *I believe we are what we eat, what we think, what we create, and what we believe.*

Are *you* in denial? Denial is very sneaky and manifests in so many ways. We sabotage our health when we eat unhealthy foods or acquire unhealthy habits. A lot of these unhealthy habits are unconscious behaviors that keep being repeated. Please don't judge yourself! Until we become conscious or aware of what lies beneath that denial, we probably will keep denying, and doing the same thing, over and over.

All those excuses we so often use…"I don't have the time"…"I've tried it before and gained all my weight back"…"Oh well, I'll just start my diet (or exercise program) tomorrow". How many *tomorrows* have you experienced as of today? For some people, that tomorrow never comes, or it arrives so many times that they eventually give up. At this point, you may begin denying that you are in denial. If you do, you are in good company. Until you can chip away at the denial layer and feel the emotions underneath it, this is a common response.

If you repress denial, it will re-surface in a different way. Our feelings are multi-layered, and this denial is more than likely camouflaging one or several more feelings that *need* to stay hidden, because you are afraid of bringing them to the surface, and as long as they are kept in the dark, you feel safe.

We need to shed some light on this denial, and embrace both the dark and light sides of our spirits. When we begin to bring light into the darkness, we experience a shift of energy, a physical lightness (pun fully intended), and this process allows room for more light. How do I know? Because I've experienced this personally, so I know it works!

Reflection:

To become aware of what lies beneath that denial, just sit still for a moment…and take a few deep breaths. Take your time, just relax, and feel your feet planted firmly on the floor. Keep focusing on the rhythm of your breath, and when you feel ready, drop your attention to your heart. Ask your heart:

- ♥ What am I denying?
- ♥ Where is the denial located in my physical body?
- ♥ What feelings are feeding my denial?
- ♥ What is my pay back for holding onto my denial?
- ♥ Am I willing to release my denial to this issue?
- ♥ Am I willing to let it go…now?

Keep breathing and focusing. Do not force the answer. Be patient. If any thoughts try to interfere, let them float away, just focus on your heart, and let the answer bubble up.

The answer may not surface immediately; it may take a few times to be successful. But with love and gentleness, the answer will rise when you are ready. Write down anything that pops into your mind, including a picture or a word. It may not make sense right away, but chances are you will begin to see a pattern once you write it down.

If you cannot release your denial now, then make a promise to yourself to release it later. Set a time and date on your calendar. Denial is such a strong resistance when you try to make changes in your life. As with any other emotional resistance, it will keep popping up in your life until you address it and move through it. Don't judge yourself or your progress; you will know when the time is right for you.

Thank your heart for being there for you, for beating every minute of every day, without conscious effort. And thank the wise part of yourself that knows you so well, and when you are ready, open your eyes, ready to face a new day! Because even a small shift in the way you feel about denial today can begin to change your life tomorrow. You will never know until you try.

My Notes...

FAMILY TIES...THAT DON'T BIND AND GAG

I quote Erma Bombeck's line – "The family ties that bind and gag". I used to live and think this way – and I ended up feeling this way too! Be careful what you wish for. So when I began to think of my family as being just who they are, and providing me lessons to learn and to grow – they no longer gagged me! Just that switch in thinking in positive ways can really make your life simpler – and easier.

Reflection:

1. Make a list of 10 traits that you absolutely dislike in other people. Allow yourself about 5 minutes, make this easy on yourself. Don't think too much, just allow the thoughts to flow.
2. Do you have 10 traits listed? Good. I was so good at this; I actually had 12 traits on my list when I first did this exercise!
3. Now – look at your list, one trait at a time. How many of these traits are actually traits you see in yourself? Be very honest – this is not an exercise for wimps! I remember looking at my list (of 12 traits) and thinking, "Oh my, these are *my* traits". Yes, it was not a pretty sight to behold. I call this the *mirroring* exercise – because we really are mirrored reflections of one another. We really are all one.

So what does this exercise prove? I always love to simplify things, and I feel it simply indicates that other people's traits are merely reflections of our own traits. This applies to both family and strangers in our society. For example, if you can't tolerate a certain person's sarcasm, are there moments you are using sarcasm without being aware?

Take one trait at a time and see how it is reflected in your life. Try to make peace with it – release the need to use sarcasm with anyone, yourself included. The people who exhibit these traits are our best teachers in life. After all, the only person you have the power to change is yourself. Hopefully, at your next family reunion, you won't be gagging anymore.

My Notes...

I PREFER TEA PARTIES...
NOT PITY PARTIES!

I remember having tea parties with my daughters when they were young. And when I think back to that time, I feel regret that perhaps I wasn't *in the moment* quite enough. I'd love to remember more details about these events, but perhaps this is just an indication that I need to have more tea parties in my life.

When things really become stressful and overwhelm you, perhaps the immediate remedy of a Pity Party sounds great. If you feel the need to eat a liter of ice cream and wallow in your pain for a few hours, that's fine. *But don't stay there!* Do take the time to feel what is below the surface, or it will re-surface again, in a different way, called Life Lessons! So roll up your sleeves and get below that surface of pity. Your Spirit will be really thankful that you did.

Reflection:

Are you having too many pity parties? You know, the days when you feel down in the dumps, that *poor me* attitude. If you don't address the issue immediately and you use a distraction to get your spirits up again, that's fine. But promise yourself to address it in the near future.

Using distraction or repressing the emotions is akin to placing a little Band-Aid on the wound. As I mentioned earlier, that same issue will resurface, because it is camping out in your unconscious mind. It is just waiting for the right moment to burst out again, which probably won't be the right moment for you. Sooner or later, you will deal with this issue, so why not deal with it now?

When you can find a quiet moment, allow this issue to resurface in a safe place. Set aside a minimum of one hour (which may be challenging), to resolve it once and for all. Have a pen and paper ready to write or journal your thoughts on paper. Keep writing. It does not have to be perfect; it only has to be released. If you don't know what to write, then write, "I don't know what to write…" Just the process of writing this truthful statement repeatedly usually unblocks the process.

You can also begin by writing a series of "I am" statements. For example, "I am sad that I can't go to the picnic." Replace the sad statement with angry, lonely, etc. with whatever emotions pop into your mind. Don't think about it too much, you are using your subconscious thoughts to do this exercise.

When I first began journaling, I used to write about everything but the issue I needed to address! It got easier with time. Now I just get right to the issue to see what emotions are hiding below the surface.

Just review the chapter *The Queen – or King of Denial* and do the exercises there if you keep having writer's block.

Like any other practices in this book, releasing the issues takes time. Keep practicing, and soon your mind and your heart will become willing partners in this focusing game. Then you will really have a great reason for that tea party!

Well, I feel that it's time you dust off that good china (who's going to get it after you're gone anyway?) and have your own tea party – for celebration, not pity!

My Notes...

I AM MY OWN BEST FRIEND

How many of you can look in the mirror and say, "I love you". Don't be silly, you may say, I know I love myself...or do you? What about all those mixed messages we send our bodies? "I'm too fat, I'll never fit into these jeans" or even worse, "Just look at my dimply thighs, I just hate them!" Just be aware that most of us may not verbalize openly what we think about our bodies, especially men. We internalize and bottle it up, all without conscious awareness. But your thoughts are just as powerful as any of these statements; your body is listening!

So just imagine that the person reflected in that mirror is your Best Friend. Yes, she/he has been with you all your life. This person has persevered through thick and thin, has carried and supported you every day of your life. Your lungs breathe for you and your heart beats for you. You don't even have to give it a second thought, unless you become ill. That's when our bodies are given a second thought. Too late, or is it?

Just like apologizing to our best friend, our bodies, when given a chance, will forgive us for not treating it right. Very seldom it is too late to try to reverse a disease, or *dis-ease* in our body. The human body is indeed an amazing piece of engineering.

Studies of children raised without love and nurturing show that their physical and mental growth is affected, compared to those children who grow up in loving environments. Even plants thrive and blossom when spoken to in a loving manner. Imagine what loving words can do for your amazing body!

Reflection:

What types of messages do you send to your body, either out loud or through your thoughts? I encourage you to look into the mirror every day and tell yourself, "I love you". It may sound and look silly at first, and it may even sound untrue, but keep up the practice, and soon you will begin to believe it too. Your body will thank you for it.

My Notes...

CELEBRATION!

Allow yourself to celebrate your progress along your journey. By embracing an attitude of gratitude and giving love and compassion to your heart, you are ready to celebrate! This can be as simple as cranking up your favorite song and singing with it loudly and with abandon! Or dancing with freedom, just loosening up those joints and muscles! And if this doesn't seem like your *cup of tea*, then perhaps a cup of freshly brewed tea or coffee is in order. Or hot chocolate, herbal tea, or any other favorite beverage of your choice.

If you are alone, execute every step of the process with *awareness*. Become aware of the boiling liquid in your cup, enjoy the aroma before you take that first sip, give thanks to the farmers who grew the tea leaves or coffee beans, to the people who brought it to your store so you can enjoy it today. Feel the hot liquid going down your throat, and feel the warmth in your tummy. Congratulations! You've just practiced the *art of mindfulness* – bringing awareness and attention into your life.

Reflection:

How can you bring mindfulness into other aspects of your life? The answer is simple: do one thing at a time, with awareness, attention and intention. Just reflect at how many motor vehicle accidents we have on our roads today. Many of these accidents are due to what the law enforcements call *distracted driving*. These distractions can be talking on cell phones, texting, eating, applying makeup, and just general absentmindedness. How many times have you reached a destination and wondered how you got there? Does this happen in all aspects of your life, or just when you drive? Accidents happen when you are distracted and inattentive, so most accidents can be prevented. Are you going through life with no awareness in regards to your road safety (and those of others), your eating habits, fitness levels, and mental health?

Our minds tell us to multi-task, and to *do* more during our day. Our minds tell us that the more we do, the more we can accomplish and the more successful we appear to others. Really?

Studies are now proving that *being aware* of what we do rather than *doing more* actually makes us more – not less – productive. By giving our full attention and focus to the task at hand, we create less accidents, make less errors, and have a greater sense of accomplishment because the task was done with deliberate care and attention to detail. Try it for one day – and see how this works for you. And don't forget to celebrate your successes!

My Notes...

EAT YOUR WAY TO HEALTH

How do you eat your food? This is not a lecture in nutrition; it is aimed at the nourishment you give your body. How do you *feed* yourself? Millions of dollars are spent on various diets and millions of people are considered obese. So are the diets working? In the short term, the answer is *yes*, but in the long term, *no*. Research shows that over 80% of people gain the lost weight back within 2 years, and 80% of women are emotional eaters. I would also venture a good estimate that at least 75% of people attending weight loss centres are women as well.

Why is this happening? One reason for this yo-yo dieting trend is *emotional.* If the underlying emotional causes of the improper nourishment are not addressed, the weight comes back, and often more than was previously lost. So it is easy to see that most people who lose the excess weight have not addressed the underlying emotional issues that caused them to gain weight in the first place. And then they regain the weight back (and more), because of this vicious cycle. From my personal weight loss experience, I had to release trapped emotions from those safe layers of fat, which served as protection for many years. Once I dealt with the emotions (I am my own best client), the excess weight began to melt away. This sounds incredible, doesn't it?

Let's *keep it simple, spirit*, because this is the title of my book! What have we been told about increasing our fibre intake, getting more vitamins from food, preventive measures for colon cancer, breast cancer, heart disease, stroke, depression, arthritis and allergies, just to name a few of the most common dis-eases in today's society? The answer is simple: eating more vegetables and fruit! This food group provides minerals, vitamins, fibre, water, antioxidants, and fills you up so you eat less of the other foods. Take charge of your health by trying it out for yourself.

Eating healthy provides more stability of your blood sugar levels, and reduces or eliminates cravings, enhances your mood, and helps keep you positive. Eating healthy is now sometimes referred to as *clean eating*, which is using simple foods to achieving greater health; the foods you ingest are as free of processing, pesticides and preservatives as possible – as if you lived back on a farm about 75 years ago. There are many great resources on the clean eating subject, both in bookstores and on the internet. Explore which one inspires you the most.

Spices and herbs are powerhouses of nutrition, and many foods dubbed *super foods* abound in our grocery aisles. We don't need to go foraging in the forests or mountains for our food supply, so what's our barrier to greater health?

Simply put, the foods that are great for the heart are great for the rest of your body. Give your heart the foods it needs – the energy centre of your heart, the heart chakra, is nurtured with vegetables. The throat chakra is nourished with fruit. By feeding our hearts and throats with foods that nourish us with love, then the need to diet just dissolves away. It becomes a compassionate and respectful way of treating our bodies, so that they are fuelled with good nutrition and love.

Feeding yourself great from the inside shows itself on the outside. Feeding yourself right makes your sugar levels, your hormones and your moods become more stable. Add 20 to 30 minutes of moderate exercise 3 times per week, and you are off to a healthier body, mind, and spirit.

Feed your spirit right too, by releasing all those negative emotional beliefs that don't serve you anymore. You have simple tools in this book to address emotional issues that float to the surface. Review those chapters to address those issues. It is the most honorable and highest *act of self-love*. Your body, mind, and spirit will thank you!

My Notes...

MIRROR, MIRROR
ON THE WALL

What do you see when you look into the mirror? How does it make you feel? Just try to observe yourself with a sense of detachment, as if you are a salesperson looking at someone who is trying on a new outfit. Is anything bubbling up for you? What are your thoughts as you look at yourself?

More and more research is being done on the power of positive thoughts. *I believe you are what you eat, you are what you think, you are what you create, and you are what you believe*. You have the power to change your own life. It requires focus, persistence, determination, and practice. It takes time to undo all the negative conditioning that our bodies and minds have been fed all the years you have lived. Research indicates that we need five positive thoughts to counteract one negative one...hmmm...and we think between 35 and 48 thoughts per minute, or between 50,000 and 70,000 thoughts daily! So if most of your thoughts are negative...you become more negative, and vice versa. So become aware of your negative thoughts, and *without judgment*, notice how many times you can reverse them into positive thinking. It takes time to reverse this process.

Just imagine what the evil queen must have felt like when the 'mirror' told her that Snow White was the fairest of them all. What a huge blow to her ego that must have been! The difference between the evil queen and you is that you don't have to compare yourself to Snow White. In fact, please don't compare yourself to anyone at all. You were born with the marvellous body, spirit, and mind that you currently have, and you are capable of making positive changes to your own life.

Always begin with small changes, baby steps. Only attempt to change one habit at a time or it may become too challenging for you. Set yourself up from the start for success. However, some people have told me that they needed to quit smoking when they stopped drinking alcohol, because the two habits were linked very strongly, and that's perfectly fine. Just do the best you can, and take it one day at a time.

Reflection:

1. Take small steps, for example, for an exercise program, make a commitment to doing 10 minutes, three times per week if you haven't been exercising in a long time. Increase the time you exercise weekly by 5 minutes or so, until you reach 30 minutes, three times per week.
2. Chart or journal your progress. A lot of us are visual learners, we learn by seeing, or reading. A few words of encouragement, such as "Great Job" can help raise your spirits when you are not in the mood to exercise. You don't have to write a book every time you journal. It doesn't have to become a chore, just a few words, or an *affirmation*. I have the Nike logo on my bathroom mirror – "Just Do It" for motivation.
3. Celebrate your successes! Look at how far you have progressed! Celebrate with a dance party – put on some rock music and shake that booty! Or sing your praises in the shower, go for a nature walk, or go for tea with a friend.

Celebrating doesn't have to be costly or full of calories to be fully savored! Just be in the moment and breathe in the love you feel for yourself right now – into your heart. You'll be glad you did.

Note on Affirmations:

Affirmations are simple, honest statements that are stated in the present and in the first person. Repeat them as often as needed. Place them on your mirror, your fridge, and in your wallet. They may not sound true at first, but they assist in replacing the negative thoughts with positive ones. Keep trying. Here are a few examples:

I am making positive changes in my life.

I am feeling stronger and healthier.

My body is radiant and vibrant with great health.

My Notes...

HEAL YOUR RELATIONSHIP WITH YOURSELF (SPIRIT)

When people ask me how they can heal their relationships with others, I ask them how their relationship with themselves is working out. After getting over the initial shock, a lot of people inform me that it's just fine…or is it?

If you reflect back (pun fully intended) on the *Mirror, Mirror on the Wall* chapter, you will notice that the queen obviously had low self-esteem, and a very unhealthy ego! None of us want to be like this character, so you need to begin to look at your reflection with love! I imagine if plastic surgery or botox injections were a household word then as they are now, the evil queen would most likely have been a great candidate.

Plastic surgery does have its merits. Some people are seriously disfigured by fatal accidents or are born with physical deformities greatly benefit from this procedure. This is reconstructive surgery, not cosmetic surgery. But when individuals begin to use radical means to an end, such as drastic surgical procedures or rapid weight loss for purely cosmetic reasons, I find this very sad. These people lack internal love for themselves, and they try to fix their self-esteem from the outside, when what really needs fixing is inside.

So what's the catch? You need to start with yourself first – by treating yourself with love, respect, patience, and compassion. When you begin to give yourself the love and respect that you so dearly deserve, only then can you begin to extend it fully to others. You can love others even though you don't love yourself totally. But when you love, honor and respect yourself fully, the relationships with other people change drastically. You become dependent on yourself, rather than co-dependent on other people. Your relationships become *interdependent* – you have healthy relationships with others and apart from them. You release the need to be dependent on relationships, substances (drugs, alcohol and cigarettes), food, or other addictive behaviors. You *trust* yourself, because to trust is to respect and honor your Truth. When you are full of love, it easily flows into all other aspects of your life. You become a bright beacon of light, able to inspire and lead people to their own Truth. And this, my friends, is true empowerment!

Reflection:

This reflection, like the others in this book, is meant to be done with the heart. Just let your mind relax, and ask your heart for its wisdom instead. Your brain thinks, justifies and rationalizes every decision you make. On the other hand, your heart speaks with wisdom, integrity and truth. When you learn to combine *both* the mind's intelligence and the heart's wisdom, you hold the key to making informed decisions, with logic and intuition.

Imagine a scale or a thermometer, with equal increments ranging from 1 to 10. Place this image in your mind. Just take a moment to close your eyes, take a few deep breaths…inhale through your nose… and exhale through your mouth. Now ask yourself the question, "On a scale of 1 to 10, the number 10 being the greatest number, how much do I love myself in this moment?" Just let the number come up from your heart. If the number is lower than you anticipated, that's fine. Just think of it as a greater chance for improvement. There is no wrong answer here.

How can you begin the healing process? Now that you have the number of how much you love yourself, you have something to improve upon, even if your number is a 10. There are always positive ways to achieving excellence, not perfection, in some areas of your life.

Let's begin by focusing on the positive aspects of your life. In the blank note page that follows, list the strengths you possess. Focus on your *inner* strengths, such as courage, empathy, honesty and compassion. If you can't find many, just ask a good friend or your partner. Too often we focus on our weaknesses and lose track of who we really are. But our acquaintances can usually help us in this matter.

This exercise is to make you feel good about yourself, from the inside-out! By focusing on your inner strengths or spiritual core values, your confidence levels increase, and you become a much more empowered version of yourself. Keep building up that list, and repeating this exercise. Soon you will have multiple reasons to love yourself more, from the inside-out.

My Notes...

AM I HAVING FUN YET?

By this chapter, you've read more than half of this book. Congratulations! You have managed to read through some emotional, physical, mental and spiritual reflections. The whole secret of this process is to not only read it, but to *practice* and *apply* it to your life.

Remember to keep taking notes of any insights or thoughts that may pop into your mind. That's why the blank pages are placed after every chapter, so that you can make notes of the great ideas you receive. All you need is a pen – you have the paper!

If you are relatively new to the body, mind and spirit concept, then take a moment to pause and reflect how it addresses your needs. How do you feel about your spirituality? Do you think you are a spiritual being inside a physical body, or just a physical being? Have you ever given much thought to your life's purpose, or do you think you even have a purpose? Have you ever questioned what happens after you die?

The answers to these questions are not in this book. The answers you seek are inside your heart and spirit. You have the wisdom to lead your own life and manifest what you need in order to fulfill your life's purpose. You have the internal wisdom. This book offers some simple, practical directions in how to get there. There are many other psychotherapy methods I use to guide my clients; these are just a few of the simpler ones you can do yourself. You don't need to invest in a GPS; all you need is to become still and listen to your heart and spirit.

Reflection:

Remember to have *fun* along the way. Leave your expectations and judgments aside. This is a journey of self-discovery and self-love. You need to take an emotional vacation from the noise and chatter of your logical mind to receive guidance from your heart. In stillness, whether it is during meditation or a nature walk, you begin to connect with what your heart desires, and to your intuition.

Allow the emotions to rise up and out. There is no easy shortcut to emotional healing. By moving through the emotions (not repressing them or dodging around them), you begin to face your old belief system and take responsibility for your life. You begin to realize that you alone are accountable for the thoughts you create and the actions that manifest. By unpacking all that emotional baggage, your suitcases begin to feel lighter, and you allow more joy into your life. This process all begins with you!

If you need to, read a chapter over again to ensure you understand what it means. The reading is simple and short, to allow you time to do it this way. Make time to take a breather and reflect on what issues still need your attention or focus. Feel free to contact me if you need to, and we can schedule a private session in person, by phone, or by Skype. The choice is yours.

The following chapter is on laughter, so you can tap into that fun energy. Remember, life is a journey, not a race to the finish line!

My Notes...

LAUGHTER...WHERE DID YOU GO?

Do you remember the first time you met your partner, your best friend, or a colleague? Do you remember laughing and joking with them, and just having a great time? And do you still have laughter and joy in your relationship?

One of the first things to enter a relationship is laughter. When we fall in love, we are giddy, we find everything becomes magnified: our senses are heightened, the grass looks greener, and we feel lighter, and more alive. We become wrapped up in a child-like energy, and as a result, we laugh more too.

Speaking of children, research varies on the number of times that a 5-year-old child laughs. Some reports indicate between 300 to 400 times a day; and adults laugh less than 20 times per day. The real value to note here is that we really do not laugh enough, never mind what the numbers indicate! Obviously children know how to laugh.

When a relationship gets stale, one of the first things to leave is laughter. Obviously, there are underlying issues that depress the joy and laughter. Often times, there is fear...of not having enough and not being enough...to our partner, but mostly to ourselves.

When we feel secure and grounded in our life, it carries over into all aspects of our lives. Whichever way we treat ourselves, we will extend that same treatment to others. So the laughter is key to bringing back that joy and abandon we see in happy children. Remember that it is hurtful to *laugh at* both others and ourselves, but it is acceptable to *laugh with* ourselves. For example, it is fine to laugh when we do something silly, but without judgment, criticism and hurtful comments or words. It is very hurtful when we direct hurtful words at ourselves, because this energy is very negative and repressive.

Reflection:

Take a moment to just sit, to bring back that light, joyful energy into your mind and body. Think of a very funny event in your past that involved you and your partner or other person in your life. Try to remember as many details as possible, with all your senses. Or think of a funny scene in a movie; this will do just fine. Just remember... let it unfold like a movie in your mind. Let it tickle your funny bone, and bring this memory down into your heart. Feel it permeate your heart, and embrace the joy and laughter of that funny memory. Just relax and breathe...let it flow through you, like a warm, gentle breeze on a summer day. Let the emotions rise up from your heart into your throat, and let them flow...whatever happens is just fine... keep breathing...Hopefully this exercise will allow you to remember and experience the joy of laughter in your heart.

If you are unable to bring up funny moments, please do not judge yourself. Try spending an hour in an amusement park, or at a water park, watching children laughing and squealing with joy, and focus on bringing this joyful energy into your own heart. Or visit a zoo or a pet store and enjoy the animals performing their antics. Or invite a friend over to watch a funny movie (a friend who has an infectious laugh). Hopefully one of these will bring more laughter and joy into your heart.

My Notes...

GOD, SOURCE, OR HIGHER POWER DID NOT LEAVE THE BUILDING!

Unlike Elvis, God, Source, or Higher Power is still very much present in our lives! We are the ones who left the building and shut the door on our spirituality when we feel alone. When you begin to feel as if the whole world has abandoned you, perhaps it is time for you to reconnect to your Source of love, which is inside your heart.

Our spirituality is a very individual aspect of being a human. I believe that we are spirits in a human body. When we become disillusioned with our physical existence on earth, it is because our Spirit is not being attended to, and it is not being nurtured. Today is a step in the right direction of your life.

Remember that saying: "God helps those who help themselves"? We need to be aware of what is happening in our own lives, and to notice when things shift inside our body, mind and spirit. It is our responsibility to do this for ourselves, because then we become active participants in our lives instead of sitting on the sidelines. Do the very best you can in any situation, and when you feel satisfied that you have done your best, release it to Source so it can manifest in your life. Today you have done your best. Today you have released it to Source.

So do the homework, do the very best you can, and when you are ready, release it! Release it to God, Source, Higher Power, the Angels, the Universe, or to whomever you wish, without any attachment to the outcome. You have to let go of your pre-conceived notion that things will turn out just as *you* planned. This is the toughest part of this exercise. *It involves letting go of the need to control exactly how things will occur in your life.* Or perhaps how you think they *should* occur. You also have to realize that sometimes, Source's answer is *No!* And if it is no, then trust that this Divine Plan is unfolding exactly as it should, and a similar or better solution is on its way.

A person's spirituality embodies their Inner Child, which is that emotional part of us that is creative, fun, and insightful. It is that inner spark that contains the wisdom and knowledge of our happiness. By tapping into our Spirit, we re-connect to that part of ourselves that makes us feel alive…and connected to our Source. Because this connection is integral to our well-being as a whole, this connection makes us remember who we are, and what our purpose is…we just have to open the door to be reminded.

When we are ready to connect to our internal Source of power, which is also where our playful, emotional Inner Child lives, we can begin to release what doesn't belong there, and fill it with joy and purpose. The following chapter has the tool for you to apply to your life.

Reflection:

Did you notice anything that was stirring up inside you as you read this chapter? I hope so, because it may indicate that your internal beliefs are shifting! Please take a moment to write your thoughts, insights, and little 'aha' moments.

We tend to pray to our Source when we are in need, but I feel we need to pray when we *don't* need assistance as well. I pray every day in some way or another. I send prayers to sick people, I send prayers to loved ones, and I pray for those people who have hurt me in some way. Huh? Yes, I need to pray and forgive those people who have betrayed or hurt me, because it releases my attachment to them. A lot of those hurtful people do not even realize they have done anything wrong. It frees your mind, body, and spirit of this blocked negative energy. Only forgive when you are ready and able to do so.

The next chapter, *Shhh…Are You Listening?* is placed immediately following this chapter to assist you in connecting with your Source.

"Don't carry a grudge. While you're carrying a grudge, the other guy's out dancing." – Buddy Hackett

My Notes...

SHHH... ARE YOU LISTENING?

I am quite sure that most of you have heard about the power of prayer. And sometimes the answer is no, as I have explained in the previous chapter. My question to you at this point would be: *how will you know when your prayer is answered*? If you go about your days with no awareness, how will you know when what you want has arrived? Will your answer have jingle bells ringing out over your rooftop? Of course not! So we have to *listen,* by being quiet and still.

I am referring to meditation. By this point, I may already have some scowls or complaints from you. Not again, you may mutter. As the British saying goes, "Stiff upper lip!", and I will explain the process.

For those of you regularly meditating, keep up the great work! Research shows there are many health benefits to meditation. And research also varies on exactly how many thoughts we have per day. My research indicated that we have between 50,000 and 70,000 thoughts per day, give or take a few; of these, 80% are negative thoughts, and 98% are the same thoughts we had the previous day. It seems as if we keep recycling old, negative thoughts and beliefs.

So just take a few minutes by being still for just a few minutes per day is like taking a mini-vacation. Your brain will thank you for it!

Most beginners find it challenging to empty their minds and to focus on their breath. The most common complaint is that their thoughts keep interrupting, so they try to resist and push them away. I have one word of advice: *don't!* The more you resist the thoughts, the more thoughts pop up…remember how many thoughts you have per day? Just let them pass by, float them away, and always promise to come back when you are done, or they may keep trying to interrupt.

Reflection:

It is often said that when we pray we connect to our Source; when we become still and silent, we hear the answer. Start with 10 minutes when you begin to meditate, and increase the time gradually. You may sit on a yoga mat, but if flexibility is an issue for you, sit in a comfortable chair with your spine straight but relaxed, to let the energy flow easily. This is a loving way of honoring the needs of your body. From this position, place both feet on the floor, and the palms of your hands facing upwards, resting on your lap. I don't encourage lying down, because you become prone to falling asleep! Please drink some water afterwards to assist the flow of energy.

The methods of meditation are varied, but just keep it simple! Focus on the rhythm of your breath, as you inhale and exhale. Inhaling through your nose and exhaling through your mouth triggers the relaxation response in your body. This breathing pattern is repeated from the Attitude of Gratitude chapter. Be patient with yourself, it may take you more than one session to relax. Keep trying.

Before you begin, you may light a candle, and focus softly (eyes half closed) on the candle, or a pleasant image. Or use a *mantra*, such as OM (pronounced *a-oo-m*, the A is sounded like the *A* in *car*), or use a simple word, such as Relax, Love, Peace, or whatever comes to mind. Just let the other 49,999 thoughts just float away for now…

and reflect on the question you want answered right now, before you begin. Write it down.

Begin with this breath, and it will bring your focus into becoming calmer and still. After 3 breaths, you may continue this breathing pattern, or just breathe your normal rhythm, whichever way is more comfortable for you.

Use a 4-second count for each intake and each release of breath and hold 4 seconds between each breath. Inhale through your nose and exhale through your mouth.

1. To a count of 4 seconds: Begin by taking 1 deep breath through your nose, into your belly (see your belly rise up), slowly up, until you completely fill up your lungs.
2. Hold the breath for 4 seconds.
3. To a count of 4 seconds, release your breath through your mouth, from the top of your lungs, and lastly from your belly, expelling all the air.
4. Hold for 4 seconds. Repeat 3 times, from step #1.

Write down any insights, words, or pictures that come into your mind.

My Notes...

MY INNER CHILD IS HAVING A TANTRUM!

When I first connected with my Inner Child, I was very grateful to be meeting that tender part of myself. I felt she had indeed been neglected and needed nurturing and love much as my own children had required while growing up (and still do as adults)! My Inner Child was wise beyond her years, and loved to be creative, playful and passionate about life. And then I experienced her first tantrum.

I felt as if I was possessed by this little rebellious energy that was putting her foot down. I literally stopped in my tracks, and thought... what the heck is going on? I knew it was my Inner Child, because my posture, my language, and even my thinking imitated a child, not an adult.

Needless to say, I attended to this part of myself immediately, because apparently to resist it was quite futile and did not quiet the tantrum, or inner turmoil. Something just didn't *feel* quite right. So I sat still, closed my eyes, and asked my Inner Child what she needed, and I received my message immediately. I was getting much too *serious*, and it was time for play. I love to dance to loud rock music, so I cranked up the music and began dancing around the room with a teddy bear!

After a few minutes of creative play and dancing, my Adult was content to sit down to creative writing and working on the business at hand, because my Inner Child was satisfied. Of course, you may go for a nature walk, build a snowman, or any other activity you did as a child.

Reflection:

Are you nurturing your Inner Child? In my experience, most people do not even realize they have an Inner Child. We grow into adulthood and we become serious with the responsibilities of life, and forget to play.

I recommend that everyone invite their Inner Child to play on a daily basis for a few minutes, or at least weekly. Schedule more time for playtime and downtime in your life. Then you can get back to being a responsible Adult. That Inner Child of yours will be very grateful that you did, and avoid the need for attention by having a tantrum!

My Notes...

HERE COMES THE JUDGE!

How influential is your judge? Mine just happened to be *huge*! All those negative beliefs that I learned as a child came flooding back – as insights! Now I know where they originated, and now I can make good use of them too.

Sometimes the Judge is called the Inner Critic. Its role is to alert us to anything we might do that can cause us harm – like jumping off the CN Tower without a parachute, but sometimes less dramatic, like eating a whole chocolate cake in one sitting by ourselves. And our Inner Critic will come in and warn us of impending doom – of a high caloric intake – and we feel shame for having even had such a thought.

I'll share my current decision-making process: I filter a great idea thought through my logical brain, and bring it down into my heart space. At about this time, the Judge comes knocking! I hold him off until I can see if the logic and intuition match up. If they do, my Judge is sent off for his nap. This is my simple and effective way I use to make informed decisions.

Reflection:

How big is your Judge? Do you feel as if you are being judged for every decision your make? Does this prevent you from moving forward in life? Does your judge remind you of old messages you heard as a child? By judging yourself, you also unconsciously extend an open invitation to letting others judge you as well. If you feel people are judging you, take time to reflect on how much you judge yourself.

Sit still for a few minutes, take a few deep breaths, and ask your Judge what it needs to tell you. Your Judge has probably been with you for a long time, and likely has your best interest in mind. But your judge does not have to rule your life anymore! Just let your brain ask your heart what it needs, and let the magic happen! Then feel free to send your Judge for a well-deserved nap.

"The intellect has little to do on the road to discovery. There comes a leap in consciousness, call it intuition or what you will, and the solution comes to you, and you don't know how or why." - Albert Einstein

My Notes...

R-E-S-P-E-C-T... ARETHA FRANKLIN SANG IT BEST!

Do you sometimes believe that other people do not respect you enough? Do you feel that you are not getting the respect you deserve, by your peers, your family, or your work colleagues? If your answer is *no*, feel free to skip this chapter altogether. If you answered *yes* to one or to both questions, then go on to the next paragraph (do not pass GO, and do not collect $200). You probably want to change this pattern of behavior as soon as possible.

I will ask you one more question: *Do you respect yourself?* If you answer a resounding *yes* to this question, then please read the first paragraph again. Your mind may be thinking that respect must be earned. Yes and no. *Respect begins and ends with you.* You must learn to respect yourself, so that you can extend it to others, and they will reciprocate it back to you. What goes around comes around.

Let's take a dog, for example. You love your dog, so you give it proper nourishment, exercise and a good home. You brush his coat and talk to him in a loving manner. And in return, your dog reciprocates with unconditional love and attention, wet kisses, and respect for you, his owner.

The same thing happens with our spirits. If we lovingly tend to the needs of our *whole* self: physical, mental, emotional and spiritual, we are showing the highest respect for ourselves. And when you respect yourself, it becomes very visible to others as well. By unconsciously raising the bar of respect for yourself, you become an example of loving power in action. When you really respect yourself, you treat yourself with loving kindness, much like that unconditional relationship with your dog. It begins on the inside and reflects on the outside. Others are drawn to show you the same respect you bestow upon yourself.

Reflection:

In what ways do you show respect to yourself? Can you relate some ways perhaps you don't respect yourself? Do you have some unhealthy habits you could change for the better? If your health is quite good, are there ways you could tweak your habits so your health improves even more? How is your mental and emotional health? How are your coping skills when dealing with stress? We are all works in progress, and we can always improve ourselves in simple but effective ways.

It takes patience, disciple and practice to change old habits and beliefs. The rule of thumb is approximately 21 days to adapt a new habit; I usually allow myself 30 days, so make sure the new habit is well established. Take life one day at a time, and if you make a mistake, don't judge yourself for being human, just begin anew right away. Forgive yourself for regressing, and keep forging ahead, no excuses. Respect yourself by treating yourself with love and forgiveness, and others will too.

I encourage you to read any chapter in this book over again which may assist you in gaining more respect for yourself. Build on your strengths, embrace that Inner Child, remember what passions you in life, and live your life with more purpose, focus, and awareness. By learning to love, nurture and forgive yourself for any mistakes, the respect will begin to flow naturally into your life.

My Notes...

THEODORE THE THERAPY BEAR

During my psychotherapy training, the instructors recommended we purchase a soft doll or teddy bear for our own therapeutic healing. I purchased a very soft, light brown teddy bear which I named Theodore, otherwise known as Teddy (I like to simplify things). He has a red bow around his neck, small black eyes, a tiny black nose, and a rounded belly. His arms are outstretched, as if he is always offering a hug. The name Theodore is bilingual, and seems to suit him rather well. By purchasing Theodore, I was making a donation to a woman's shelter. When our eyes first met at the store, let's just say he was a perfect match for my Inner Child.

Theodore knows all my secrets (I told my husband not to feel jealous). Many times when I was experiencing the roller coaster ride of emotions, I would reach for Theodore and he always seemed to understand. I never felt judged, criticized, or mocked when I expressed my heartfelt emotions. And he was always there with open arms, ready to give me a warm, furry hug.

At this point, you probably think I was, or I am quite silly! Well, it is my professional opinion that if more people bought teddy bears, and used them as therapy bears much like I did (and still do), there would be a lot more peace, love and joy in today's society, and a lot less hatred, addictions and wars. So go out and buy a teddy bear, in the name of world peace!

Reflection:

When we have decisions to make or changes to manifest in our lives, the use of props such as therapy bears can assist us in the process. We access the little child in our hearts, called the Inner Child, when we use this method. Most of the wounding to our spirits that still affects us today occurred in childhood, and was repressed to avoid pain. Take a moment to reflect on these words, and write what your Inner Child is inviting you to do. Who knows, perhaps you will invest in a teddy bear!

My Notes...

ARE WE THERE YET?

I distinctly remember one or both daughters piping up from the back seat of our vehicle, only minutes from home, "Are we there yet?" This innocent statement was as welcoming to my ears as nails on a chalkboard, especially if the destination was still 12 hours away!

In the body, mind, and spiritual healing processes, I feel we are never quite 'there'. Every day we deal with life the best we can. We all are in the process of changing, recycling, and adapting to different ways of dealing with our issues. Hopefully, along the way we choose new and improved ways to cope with life's challenges and turn them into opportunities for learning and growth. We learn from our mistakes and move onto the next stage of our process.

I believe that life challenges present us with lessons we need to learn so our spirits and souls will expand and grow. I also believe there are no coincidences, and the 'chance' circumstances do not happen by chance at all, but they are all part of a Divine plan. Your beliefs may be different from mine, and that is perfectly fine.

Reflection:

So if we are not there yet, then where are we? I feel we are always a part of the process we call change, or life transitions. We are born; we grow into adolescence, then adulthood, and then eventually our physical body returns to the earth. If you look at it from this perspective, we become recycled material! What are your thoughts or beliefs on this issue? Try to visualize how far you've come by writing down what you have accomplished, and what opportunities arose out of your challenges, and be grateful for not being there yet. Make an attempt to see the silver lining in the dark clouds; it goes unnoticed unless you open your eyes to the possibilities.

My Notes...

THE LITTLE SPIRIT
THAT CAN...

At this point in the book, you have hopefully gained insights from the reflections in each section. And hopefully you are beginning to know yourself better, which is what many of my clients state as one of their goals: to know themselves better. As I've mentioned in the body of this book, we are human beings, not human doings, and yet we keep ourselves busy with doing more and more. I hope this book has given you a taste of what *being* feels like, even if it just means a few minutes of reflection.

I have faith in the human spirit that it has the capacity and capability to heal itself when given the right tools and techniques. I have worked with persons who have mild to severe physical and mental disabilities, and they are very selective with whom they wish to interact. Even my clients who cannot speak for themselves have a very real sense of what they need. I know they are highly sensitive to energy and sound, and gravitate towards individuals who connect with them on their heart level. Their spirit seems drawn to people who are open and allow this to occur.

I believe your Little Spirit can experience more freedom if you allow it to do so. To shut off the flow of breath and to close down your heart energy is, in my opinion, not living to your full extent. You were meant to feel and experience life in all its glory. By moving through your minor life events with more ease and grace, you will gain more confidence in navigating through the major transitions.

Reflection:

When your Adult Spirit allows your Little Spirit to play and be creative, the magic happens! Your Little Spirit (or Inner Child) knows how to be silly and have fun. Don't let your Little Spirit have a tantrum before you acknowledge its existence – remember to schedule time in your busy life for play. There is plenty of time to be the serious and responsible Adult Spirit. Remember to always have your Adult Spirit at the wheel of your life, while your Little Spirit is a passenger in the back seat, saying, "Wheee…I know I can." Take the time now to schedule at least one half hour a week on your calendar. Then move up to once per day. It takes time to get fun back into your life, one day at a time.

My Notes...

DEBUTANTE PARTY!

During the last months of my psychotherapy training, I expressed my concerns to one of my instructors about stepping out into the world. He looked at me and said, "Why don't you just think of yourself as a debutante?" I loved it! I immediately visualized myself wearing an elegant pink princess dress with long white gloves. This image certainly was a lot more pleasant than the images that I'd previously had in mind.

How are *you* stepping out into the world? How do you show up in your own life? It is so crucial to make time for your mental, emotional, physical and spiritual aspects of yourself. Begin making yourself a priority in your life, because no one else will. As an adult, you have responsibilities, but you still need to be accountable for all aspects of *your* wellness.

For example, by connecting with your Inner Child, your Spirit, you empower yourself to change the things that are not working for you now, as an adult. If you feel your parents were not supportive when you were a child, then you need to become a parent to your Inner Child. Show yourself some love and nurturing, with positive actions and words.

You cannot change the past, but with simple tools as demonstrated in this book, you can begin to re-program your brain into positive methods of thinking and doing life events. You are able to change how you *respond* to life events, rather than *react* to them. When you shed some emotional baggage to your past life, this also flows into the mental, physical and spiritual aspects of your life.

Also take back your power by giving back the unclaimed baggage to those people who try to push their stuff onto you. Don't get into other people's drama, and if you do, then do your spirit a great favour: stop and look at why you tend to have this behavior. If you want peace and joy into your life, begin releasing your own emotional baggage, and let others tend to their own. Each and every one of us owes it to our spirits. I wish you abundant blessings on your journey.

Chris, this is *our* debutante party! You led me through my case study supervisions with intuition and grace. As I write these words in this last chapter, I feel your presence. Thank you for your pearls of wisdom. Rest in peace, Chris. Namaste.

My Notes...

EPILOGUE

I believe that most of the attitudes and behaviors you exhibit in your daily life stems from a lack of connection to your own Inner Child, or Spirit, as I refer to in *Keep It Simple, Spirit*. I believe that once that true connection is remembered and applied in your life, you will gain a greater sense of belonging and purpose in the world.

All I ask is that you become present to your own life. You have been granted the gift of life – how will you use the remainder of it? Hiding behind a shield is exhausting, and shedding all those layers of emotional baggage is exhilarating! Choose to become an active player in your own healing journey. Honor your passions, your gifts, and your Spirit.

I wish you abundant blessings of Peace, Love, and Joy. Thank you for reading Keep It Simple, Spirit.

THE SNOWFLAKE

Like the snowflake
We are all different and unique
Every one of us has special qualities
We all have gifts to share with the world

To deny these gifts and keep them hidden
Is to deny our very existence
Our purpose for living
And our mission in life

Summon up your courage
Move through your fears
Call upon your Higher Spirit
Show your gifts to the world
Your time has come.

- Connie Robichaud (February 19, 2014)

BIBLIOGRAPHY

Emotional Eating
by Marcelle Pick, OB/GYN NP

When You Lose Weight – And Gain it All Back, Women's Health
by Gretchen Voss

There Are 50,000 Thoughts Standing Between You and Your Partner Every Day!
by Bruce Davis, Ph.D.

Are You Meeting Your Laugh Quota?
Why You Should Laugh Like A 5-Year-Old
Published on June 21, 2011
by Dr. Pamela Gerloff in The Possibility Paradigm

CPSIA information can be obtained at www.ICGtesting.com
Printed in the USA
BVOW05s0514220514

354224BV00001B/15/P